THE GREAT MIGRATION

AN AMERICAN STORY
PAINTINGS BY JACOB LAWRENCE
with a poem in appreciation by Walter Dean Myers

The Museum of Modern Art, New York • The Phillips Collection • HarperCollinsPublishers

This is the story of an exodus of African-Americans who left their homes and farms in the South around the time of World War I and traveled to northern industrial cities in search of better lives. It was a momentous journey. Their movement resulted in one of the biggest population shifts in the history of the United States, and the migration is still going on for many people today.

The great migration is a part of my life. I grew up knowing about people on the move from the time I could understand what words meant. There was always talk in my house of other families arriving from the South. My family was part of the first big wave of the migration, which occurred between the years 1916 and 1919. My mother was born in Virginia, and my father was born in South Carolina. Somehow they met on their way north, and I was born in Atlantic City, New Jersey, in 1917. We settled for a while in Philadelphia. Many other families settled there, too, but many traveled even farther, to Pittsburgh, New York,

Chicago, Detroit, Cleveland, and St. Louis.

I arrived in New York City's Harlem community in 1930, when I was thirteen years of age. Harlem was crowded with newcomers, but we all settled in somehow. I went to school, and after school I went to an arts-and-crafts program at the Utopia Children's House, which my mother enrolled me in to keep me busy while she was at work. I decided then that I wanted to be an artist. When I first started painting, I was just making designs. The colors and patterns that decorated my mother's apartment influenced my pictures. Later I started painting street scenes. I painted peddlers, parades, fire escapes, apartment houses—all that was new to me.

Eventually, teachers, friends, even actors on the street corners helped me to understand how my own experiences fit into a much larger story—the history of African-Americans in this country. It seemed almost inevitable that I would tell this story in my art. I spent many hours at the Schomburg Library in Harlem reading books about the great migration, and I took notes. Soon my re-search gave me the images I needed to tell the story of the great migration. Many of the images were new for me—along with my street scenes, I would now need to paint rural landscapes, images of violence, and interiors, like the inside of a schoolroom.

I started the **Migration** series in 1940, when I was twenty-two years old, and finished it one year later. I can still remember all the panels spread out in my studio on tables made from boards and sawhorses. My wife, **Gwen,** helped me to prepare the surfaces. I painted the panels all at once, color by color, so they share the same palette. I had made some preparatory sketches that provided me with general outlines, but I worked out the details of the pictures as I painted them. There are sixty panels in the series, and since I wanted them to tell a story, I gave each one a number and painted it directly onto its frame.

To me, migration means movement. While I was painting, I thought about trains and people walking to the stations. I thought about field hands leaving their farms to become factory workers, and about the families that sometimes got left behind. The choices made were hard ones, so I wanted to show what made the people get on those northbound trains. I also wanted to show just what it cost to ride them. Uprooting yourself from one way of life to make your way in another involves conflict and struggle. But out of the struggle comes a kind of power, and even beauty. I tried to convey this in the rhythm of the pictures, and in the repetition of certain images.

"And the migrants kept coming" is a refrain of triumph over adversity. **My** family and others left the South on a quest for freedom, justice, and dignity. If our story rings true for you today, then it must still strike a chord in our American experience.

Jacob Lawrence, 1992

Around the time I was born, many African-Americans from the South left home and traveled to cities in the North in search of a better life. My family was part of this great migration.

There was a shortage of workers
in northern factories because many
had left their jobs to fight in the
First World War.

The factory owners had to find new workers to replace those who were marching off to war.

Northern industries offered southern blacks jobs as workers and lent them money, to be repaid later, for their railroad tickets. The northbound trains were packed with recruits.

Nature had ravaged the South. Floods ruined farms.
The boll weevil destroyed cotton crops.

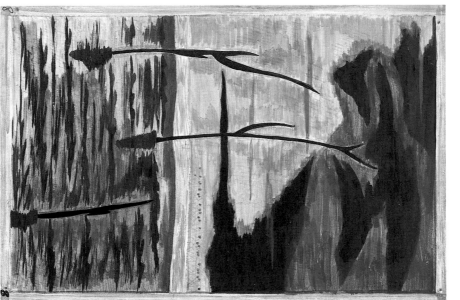

The war had doubled the cost of food, making life even harder for the poor.

Railroad stations were so crowded with migrants that guards were called in to keep order.

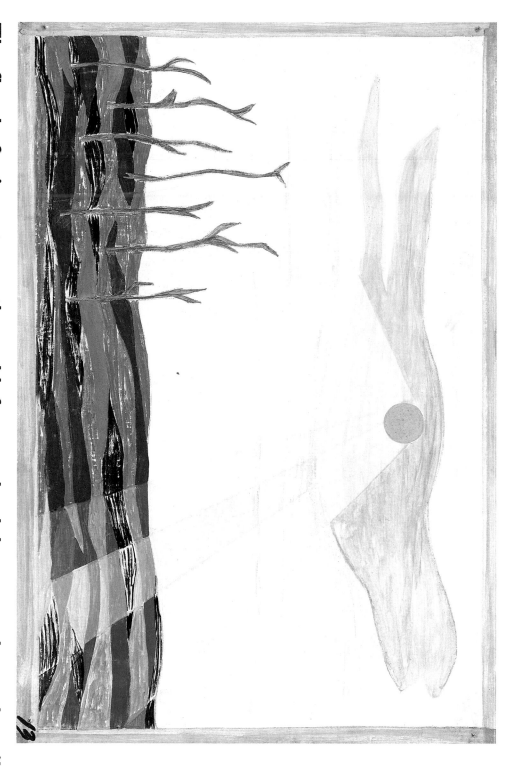

The flood of migrants northward left crops back home to dry and spoil.

For African-Americans the South was barren in many ways. There was no justice for them in the courts, and their lives were often in danger.

Although slavery had long been abolished, white landowners treated the black tenant farmers harshly and unfairly.

And so the migration grew.

Segregation divided the South.

The black newspapers told of better housing and jobs in the North.

Families would arrive very early at railroad stations to make sure they could get on the northbound trains.

20

Early arrival was not easy, because African-Americans found on the streets could be arrested for no reason.

And the migrants kept coming.

23

24

In the South there was little opportunity for education, and children labored in the fields. These were more reasons for people to move north, leaving some communities deserted.

There was much excitement and discussion about the great migration.

Agents from northern factories flocked into southern counties and towns, looking for laborers.

Families often gathered to discuss whether to go north or to stay south. The promise of better housing in the **North** could not be ignored.

The railroad stations were crowded with migrants.

Letters from relatives in the North and articles in the black press portrayed a better life outside the South.

Many migrants arrived in Chicago.

In Chicago and other cities they labored
in the steel mills . . . .

and on the railroads.

And the migrants kept coming.

Southern landowners, stripped of cheap labor, tried to stop the migration by jailing the labor agents and the migrants. Sometimes the agents disguised themselves to avoid arrest, but the migrants were often taken from railroad stations and jailed until the trains departed.

Black and white southern leaders met to discuss ways to improve conditions to stop the flow of workers north.

Although life in the North was better, it was not ideal.

Many migrants moved to Pittsburgh, which was a great industrial center at the time.

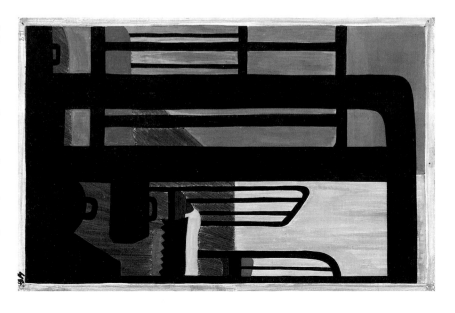

Although they were promised better housing in the North, some families were forced to live in over-crowded and unhealthy quarters.

The migrants soon learned that segregation was not confined to the South.

Many northern workers were angry because they had to compete with the migrants for housing and jobs. There were riots.

Longtime African-American residents living in the North did not welcome the newcomers from the South and often treated them with disdain.

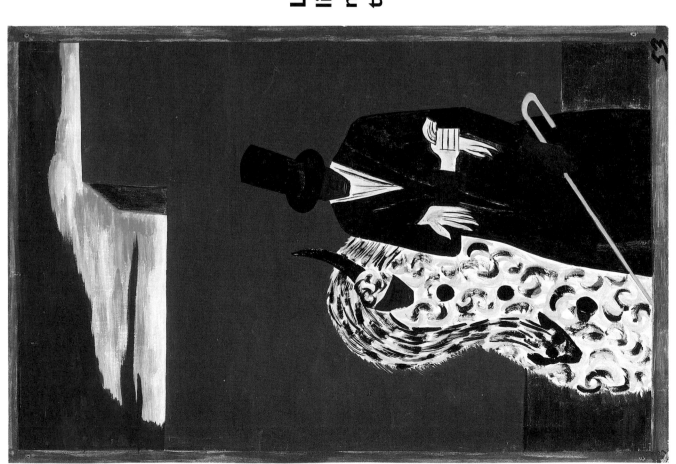

The migrants had to rely on each other. The storefront church was a welcoming place and the center of their lives, in joy and in sorrow.

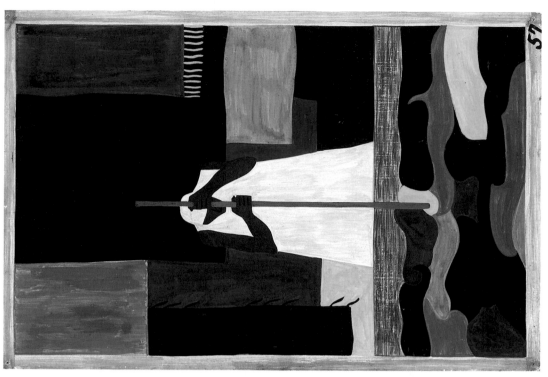

Black professionals, such as doctors and lawyers, soon followed their patients and clients north. Female workers were among the last to leave.

Life in the North brought many challenges, but the migrants' lives had changed for the better. The children were able to go to school, and their parents gained the freedom to vote.

And the migrants kept coming.

Theirs is a story of African-American strength and courage. I share it now as my parents told it to me, because their struggles and triumphs ring true today. People all over the world are still on the move, trying to build better lives for themselves and for their families.

MIGRATION

Walter Dean Myers

In the waiting room, "Colored,"
Hands, calloused and as black as the rich
Georgia/Carolina/Alabama dirt they leave behind,
Clasp and unclasp silently,
Some hold Bibles older than freedom,
Others hold food that will not last the long journey.
There is no need to speak, to explain
How so many nights of love and terror
So many back cracking, heartbreaking days
So many humbled dreams
Can fit into the small rope-tied case that sits
On the ancient hardwood floor between them

A stirring at the ticket counter
Stiffens backs, tightens stomachs
Hard-eyed men with guns in their belts
Stare daggers into the waiting room, "Colored."
In the distance the *whoo! whoo!* of the train breaks
The stillness of a forever moment
The men with guns look, shake their heads, and leave
Life goes on

The tickets to Chicago/Detroit/New York are heavy
As heavy as the memory of a church built
With sweat and faith and knotted pine
On the edge of the old burying ground

But there are the children, and there is the hope
Of a people with yet one more river to cross

Dedicated to the migrants whose struggle
for "life, liberty, and the pursuit of happiness"
is a moving story in American history

About the Artist

Jacob Lawrence was born in 1917 and grew up in New York City during the Depression. He studied art at the Harlem Workshop and the American Artists School. Mr. Lawrence is best known for several sequences of narrative paintings, including *Harriet Tubman* and *Frederick Douglass*, and for his illustration of the book *Harriet and the Promised Land*. He has won numerous awards, including the National Medal of Arts, and his work is represented in the collections of major museums.

Along with his wife, Gwendolyn Knight, Mr. Lawrence lives in Seattle, where he is Professor Emeritus at the University of Washington.

About the Poet

Walter Dean Myers is the highly acclaimed author of dozens of books for children and young adults. He has received the Coretta Scott King Award four times, and a Newbery Honor. His books have been named ALA Notables and ALA Best Books for Young Adults.

Mr. Myers lives in Jersey City, New Jersey, with his family.

About the Art

The Migration of the Negro, a narrative series of sixty individual panels, was painted between 1940 and 1941. In March 1942, less than one year after its completion, the series was divided evenly between the collections of The Museum of Modern Art, New York, and The Phillips Collection, Washington, D.C. The series was last reunited in 1971 for the exhibition *Artist as Adversary*, which was shown at both The Museum of Modern Art and The Phillips Collection. This book is published on the occasion of the 1993 exhibition *Jacob Lawrence: The Migration Series*, organized by The Phillips Collection, which will be traveling from Washington, D.C., to Milwaukee; Portland, Oregon; Birmingham; St. Louis; and New York City.

About the Book

The text of this book was set in 17 pt. Gill Sans. The paper is 80# L.O.E. Dull. The color separations and interior printing were done by Princeton Polychrome Press. The jacket was printed by New England Book Components. The book was bound by Worzalla. Book design by Tom Starace.

This book has been made possible by Osa Brown, Director of Publications, The Museum of Modern Art, New York, and by Elizabeth Hutton Turner, Associate Curator, The Phillips Collection; Jessica Altholz and David Gale, editors; Tom Starace, art director; Marc Sapir, John Vitale, and Lucille Schneider, production; Darla Decker and Elisabeth Foxley Leach, project assistants. Project consultants: George Nicholson, Gwendolyn Knight, Harriet Bee, Michael Hentges, Tim McDonough, Helen Santini, and John B. Murphy.

The Migration of the Negro. 1940–41. A series of sixty works. Tempera on gesso on composition board, each 18 x 12 inches (vertical or horizontal). The Museum of Modern Art, New York, Gift of Mrs. David M. Levy (even numbers); The Phillips Collection, Washington, D.C. (odd numbers).

Introduction based on an interview conducted by curator Elizabeth Hutton Turner, October 3, 1992, available in The Phillips Collection Archives.

Library of Congress Cataloging-in-Publication Data
Lawrence, Jacob, date
  The great migration : an American story / paintings by Jacob Lawrence.
    p.   cm.
  Summary: A series of paintings chronicles the journey of African Americans who, like the artist's family, left the rural South in the early twentieth century to find a better life in the industrial North.
  ISBN 0-06-023037-1. — ISBN 0-06-023038-X (lib. bdg.)
  ISBN 0-06-023453-9 (limited edition)
  ISBN 0-87070-166-5 (MoMA)
  ISBN 0-943044-20-0 (The Phillips Collection)
  1. Lawrence, Jacob, date—Juvenile literature.   2. Afro-Americans in art—Juvenile literature.   3. Rural-urban migration in art—Juvenile literature.   [1. Afro-Americans—History.   2. Lawrence, Jacob, date—Family.   3. Artists.]   I. Title.
ND237.L29A4   1993
759.13—dc20   93-16788
                                                                               CIP
                                                                               AC
2   3   4   5   6   7   8   9   10